ROBIN GILBERT

LEADERSHIP CONCEPTS

**The Essential Guide to Effective Leadership,
Discover Different Concepts and Approach On
How to Become a Better Leader**

Descrierea CIP a Bibliotecii Naţionale a României
ROBIN GILBERT
   LEADERSHIP CONCEPTS. The Essential Guide to Effective Leadership, Discover Different Concepts and Approach On How to Become a Better Leader / Robin Gilbert – Bucharest: Editura My Ebook, 2021
   ISBN

ROBIN GILBERT

LEADERSHIP CONCEPTS

**The Essential Guide to Effective Leadership,
Discover Different Concepts and Approach On
How to Become a Better Leader**

My Ebook Publishing House
Bucharest, 2021

CONTENTS

INTRODUCTION TO LEADERSHIP

Napoleon once said: "One bad general does better than two good ones." It takes a moment for the sense of this to register, but it is the same as our modern saying that "too many cooks spoil the broth". Having one set of instructions, even if they are flawed, is preferable to having two sets of perfect directions that, when enacted together without reference to each other, cause havoc.

This is the principle of leadership in a nutshell. It is all about maintaining focus and creating positive outcomes.

The same can be applied to individuals who strive to become leaders. There needs to be focus and determination.

Advice can be given, but does not have to be heeded. History is full of leaders whose beginnings were disastrous, and had they listened to the naysayers of this world, the world would be a poorer place today.

Leadership can be learned. Some people are certainly born with leadership skills, but this is not a prerequisite for becoming a leader. More important is dedication to the art of leadership. Leadership involves understanding how to inspire, influence and control how people behave. It is not a simple matter of shouting, or having a deep and booming voice; or being great in physical stature; Gandhi possessed none of these attributes, but managed to lead a nation and inspire millions around the world.

Sometimes, leadership may be no more than having a poignant message for a receptive audience at an opportune moment. Of itself, leadership is neither good nor bad; the world has known more than its fair share of evil and charismatic dictators.

In the world of business, the perception of leadership has changed from its early days when it largely mirrored the military model of leadership from the top down, with powerful individuals dominating large groups of less powerful people.

Nowadays, leadership in business is far more knowledge-driven. The lowliest employee may end up effectively leading the direction of a vast corporation through his or her innovative ideas. Anyone with critical knowledge can show leadership. This is known as thought-leadership. In other situations, leadership can be about taking a stand for what you believe in, and trying to convince people to think and act differently.

Leadership has been variously described as the "process of social influence in which one person can enlist the aid and support of others in the accomplishment of a common task"; "creating a way for people to contribute to making something extraordinary happen"; "the ability to successfully integrate and maximize available resources within the internal and external

9

environment for the attainment of organizational or societal goals"; and "the capacity of leaders to listen and observe, to use their expertise as a starting point to encourage dialogue between all levels of decision-making, to establish processes and transparency in decision-making, to articulate their own values and visions clearly but not impose them. Leadership is about setting and not just reacting to agendas, identifying problems, and initiating change that makes for substantive improvement rather than managing change".

There is truth to all of the above definitions, but they all apply to the *ideals* of leadership.

So what of leadership gone awry?

UNDERSTANDING THE DARK SIDE

The dark side of any individual when allowed to go unchecked can create a rigid and dysfunctional personality that stifles creativity, and taints or ruins relationships. When such characteristics are given reign in a leader, a self- righteous and bombastic person can result, who alienates the very people they are meant to inspire.

Compulsive leaders feel like they have to do everything themselves. They try to manage every aspect of their business, often refusing to delegate, and cannot resist having their say on everything. As they lack trust in others, they cannot let anyone else take responsibility, therefore they restrict personal growth in their team.

Compulsive leaders have many other traits. They are perfectionists who must follow highly rigid and systematized daily routines, and are concerned with status. Thus they strive to impress their superiors with their diligence and efficiency and continually look for reassurance and approval. This can lead to them becoming workaholics, and their team is viewed as failing if they don't keep pace. Spontaneity is not encouraged as this bucks the routine.

Despite this appearance of total control, such leaders can be fit to explode on the inside, and this can be the result of a childhood environment where unrealistic expectations were placed on them. Their attempts to keep control are linked to their attempts to suppress anger and resentment, which makes them susceptible to outbursts of temper if they perceive they are losing their grip.

Narcissistic leaders are focused on themselves. Life and the world revolve around them, and they must be at the center of all that is happening. Whilst they exaggerate their own merits, they will try to ignore the merits of others, or seek to devalue them, because other people's accomplishments are seen as a threat to their own standing. The worst type of narcissistic leader cannot tolerate even a hint of criticism and disagreement, and avoid their self- delusions and fantasies being undermined by surrounding themselves with sycophants.

Where possible, they will attempt to use the merits of others for their own advancement, and think nothing of stepping on people to get ahead. Their own feeling of self-importance means they are unable to empathize with those in their team, because they cannot feel any connection. Their only focus is on receiving plaudits that further bolster their sense of greatness. Such an attitude is often the result of a deep-seated inferiority complex, and thus no matter how much they are achieving, they will never feel it is enough.

Some narcissistic leaders take on a sidekick, but this person is expected to toe the line at all times, and serves only to reflect glory onto them and loudly approve of all that they do. Clever sidekicks can subtly manipulate the leader into focusing on the operational outcome of their plans, rather than just their own self-aggrandizement. Ultimately, this type of leader can be very successful if their vision is strong and they get the organization to identify with them and think like they do. Such productive narcissists have more perspective, and can step back and even laugh at their own irrational needs.

Paranoid leaders are exactly as they sound: paranoid that other people are better than they are, and thus they view even the mildest criticism as devastating. They are liable to overreact if they sense they are being attacked, especially in front of other people. This can manifest itself in open hostility.

This attitude is the result of an inferiority complex that perceives even the most constructive criticism in the wrong way. The paranoid leader will be guarded in their dealings with other people because they do not want to reveal too much of themselves in case they display their weaknesses and are attacked or undermined. They may be scared that their position is undeserved, therefore can be deeply suspicious of colleagues who may steal their limelight or perhaps challenge for their position.

This is not always a wholly negative trait, however. A healthy dose of paranoia can be key to success in business, because it helps keep leaders on their toes, always aware of opportunities not to be missed. It is the opposite end of the spectrum to being complacent, and can make for a very successful venture.

Co-dependent leaders do not enjoy taking the lead, and instead seek to copy what others have done or are doing. They avoid confrontation and would rather cover up problems than face them head-on. Planning ahead is not their forte. They tend instead to react to whatever comes their way, rather than acting to alter outcomes or achieve goals.

Codependent leaders, therefore, are not leaders at all. They are reactionary and have the habit of keeping important information to themselves because they are not prepared to act upon it. This can clearly lead to poor outcomes because all the pertinent facts are not known to those below the leader who may be charged with making decisions.

This type of leader avoids confrontation and is thus liable to accept a greater workload for themselves rather than respond negatively to any request. They are also prone to accepting the blame for situations they have not caused.

Passive-aggressive leaders feel like they need to control everything, and when they can't they cause problems for those who *are* in control. However, they are sneaky in their ploys, and are very difficult to catch out. Their main characteristics are that they can be stubborn, purposely forgetful, intentionally inefficient, complaining (behind close doors), and they parry demands put on them through procrastination.

Typically, if they feel they are not firmly in the driving seat, they will jump out and puncture the tires when no one is looking, then feign horror and pretend to search around for a tire iron.

This type of leader has two speeds: full speed ahead and stopped. When situations do not go their way, they will offer their full support for whatever has been decided, then gossip and back stab, willfully cause delays, and generally create upset. When confronted, they claim to have been misinterpreted. Passive aggressive leader are often chronically late for appointments, using any excuse to dominate and regain some control of the situation.

Dealing with passive-aggressive leaders is thus a draining and frustrating affair that saps energy. They are not averse to short outbursts of sadness or anger to regain some control, but are ultimately fearful of success since it leads to higher expectations.

HOW TO LEAD AND INFLUENCE PEOPLE

Leading people has nothing to do with managing them. Too many managers are trying to micro-manage their staff, all the while forgetting to lead them effectively.

If you want to become a strong leader you need to lead by example. This means you have to show your team that you are perfectly capable to set examples. By doing so you will earn their respect and create lifelong devotees who would move mountains to please you.

Conversely, a manager who hides behind his office door while commanding staff isn't going to gain much respect in the work place.

Ultimately the success of any business venture lies in the hands of its employees and NOT the managers. A manager's responsibility is to organize and manage business systems, systems that will see to the successful finalization of projects.

If your staff are unhappy it will soon show in their lack of productivity. This will influence your bottom line. Chances are customer complaints will start to amass and office gossip will run hot. This is counterproductive to running a well oiled machine – your business.

No organization can function for very long without the co-operation of its employees. Unfortunately, the necessity in any organization is that there are various levels of status within the team, and this can lead to conflicts if not managed properly.

The effective leader has to realize that the team under them is there because they have to be. Most employees work to earn money, not because they enjoy the daily grind of a nine-to-five.

For this reason, there must be an effort to build healthy relationships, or life in the workplace can become untenable for everyone, and productivity will decline.

Leaders need to make their workplace society function positively, with co-operation and respect. In this way everyone is working for the common good and towards a common purpose. This demands that effective relationships are built upon an understanding of each other's needs. It is no different to how things should be in the home; no personal relationship will last very long if there is a sense that one or both parties are being selfish.

The most effective way to understand how other people are feeling is to listen to what they have to say. This must be done without judging, and not as though you are being forced to do so by some higher authority. Very often, teams will have the same goals as their leaders, but may just want to know that they are not seen as automatons that have no creative input.

Quality workplace relationships make people feel happy. One of the major reasons why employees move on from a company is because of relationship clashes with leaders or other colleagues.

Leaders should also make sure that they create the circumstances for understanding within their team, and this means asking questions. Assuming that your team will simply pipe up and express their feelings is not enough; many people will not feel it is their place to speak up unless they are specifically asked to do so.

Listening should be done attentively, not glancing at your watch every couple of minutes or trying not to look bored. This means you listen without interrupting or fidgeting, and with the correct expression. Your expression, by the way, should be genuine or you will be found out very quickly and the situation will become worse than had you not asked in the first place.

A great way to foster healthy relationships with your team is by meeting them in a more social environment on regular occasions. Some companies choose to send their staff to regular golfing outings while others prefer to host a monthly BBQ or weekend trips.

Regardless what you end up choosing, the key lies in giving your team a chance to connect away from the daily grind.

Building effective relationships means that neither party must make any assumptions. As a leader, you cannot expect people to understand exactly what we want and why you want it. Sometimes it is this lack of comprehension that causes problems. As much as you must trust your team members to have intelligence, if they are not party to the goals you are working towards they can become resistant. As far as possible, your team should be conversant with your goals and how their actions are contributing to their successful outcome. Humans are inquisitive and function better when not kept in the dark.

Respect is the key ingredient of any good relationship, and this means respect for yourself as well as others. Genuinely listening and understanding are the ways in which you show that you respect the person you are talking to.

Quickly judging based on preconceived ideas or prejudice is the opposite of having respect. Bear in mind that not everyone will respond in 100% perfect fashion to all that occurs in the workplace. Although it is not the leader's job to be a permanent shoulder to cry on, it is important to accept that your team is made up of individuals whose lives may not be as perfect as their coffee-break banter might lead you to believe.

Whilst creating a healthy working relationship is a crucial goal, the smart leader will always bear in mind that conflict is inevitable and must be managed, rather than ignored for the sake of apparent peace.

Relationships can never improve unless problems are identified and confronted. Differences between people are inevitable, and hearing them aired can lead to some very useful resolutions that produce ideas beyond the expected. The alternative is highly detrimental: to let problems fester and build, and ruin the atmosphere in a workplace, if not productivity levels.

Keys for success in working relationships:

1. One party at least should value the relationship – This may start off as a one-way street, but this can lead to a meeting of minds later on.

2. Listen effectively, without judging – Listening in this way will promote mutual understanding and mutual respect.

3. Have informal chats – Chatting over a coffee can encourage a more frank exchange of views than meeting officially with a desk between you.

4. Create an open culture – Your team should know they can speak freely, no matter if that is to express happiness, joy, contentment, anger, irritation, sadness or fear. Negative feelings that are hoarded cause significant problems.

Leaders must take responsibility for their team's performance, which means leaders must be happy that the direction of their team is one which the leader thinks is best. Although it is useful to have creative sessions with team members to bat around a few ideas, the overarching goals that the team must fulfill are most often set by the leader, or some authority above the leader.

The challenge is therefore to get the team "onside" with the given aims, even when some team members may wholeheartedly disagree with them, or baulk at the idea that these have been imposed on them from above.

Despite the accepted hierarchy of any workplace, for a team to work most efficiently, its members – especially higher level ones – may want to feel they are contributing more then the spade work; they may like to feel that they have chosen where some of the plots should be dug.

This presents a challenge for the leader who cannot just let his or her subordinates have free play. The team must be made to feel involved and motivated. Or perhaps the situation is worse, and your team is beginning to show a little disobedience. How then to provoke a positive response in them?

The answer is by empowering your team, as far as possible. Short of handing over the reigns and heading off home, the motivational leader must be able to create a sense that their team is actively involved in the process and contributing in a real sense to the overall outcome of the project. This can involve learning how to make your suggestions appeal to them. This may mean you solicit their opinions and take the best ideas on board. Or you may have to convince them that your goals are shared and that their futures are tied to your overall success. It may be a simple matter of making an employee understand that their job will be safer if they perform well; reminding them that they are working for themselves and their family, and not just for a company.

However, empowering others does not just mean employing tactics that persuade other people to your own opinion or goals. It can also mean demonstrating leadership qualities that inspire others to act at their very best, no matter what is asked of them. Such leadership qualities would be most in evidence in the armed services, where the end result of potentially being killed is rarely going to elicit a whoop and a cheer. Soldiers are empowered to greatness by the examples set by their commanding officers.

Sometimes, it is just a matter of being an admirable and inspirational human being. Of course, some are born with more of these qualities than others, but we can all strive to lead by example, so that others will feel empowered to make great things happen.

GETTING THE MOST FROM YOUR TEAM

Start right

When a staff member joins your team, give them time to become fully acclimatized to your company. The sooner they settle, the sooner you can start to reap rewards. It will help if you complete an induction and a detailed contract of employment, which outlines what you expect from them.

Create expectations

Strange as it may sound, some employees do not have a clear sense of their role. Such confusion can cause arguments, or even duplication or omission of tasks. This is clearly bad for productivity. Your team needs to know their job and responsibilities; a job description will help.

Stand back

Part of empowering your team is trusting they can get on with the job without you peering over their shoulder every fifteen minutes. If you want staff members to flourish, they should be allowed to get on with their job. Of course you need to keep a watchful eye, but there is a happy medium where they know you trust them. Your team is more likely to over-perform if they feel good about what they are doing. Motivated staff work harder. Money is often not the prime motivator. They want to know what is expected of them, and then they want to be allowed to get on with it. This is far easier if the right people are employed in the first place.

Communication

Effective communication is the lifeblood of any organization, regardless of its size. That may mean face-to-face talks or pinning notes on a board.

Provided your team knows what's going on, you are being an effective leader. Try asking your team how they prefer communication to happen. This helps to empower them.

Keep communicating

It can happen that there is a sincere intention to improve communication, and it all starts off positively: team briefs, newsletters; intranets, etc. Then things start to slow down. As a leader you should not let this happen. It may mean important information is not imparted, or you are viewed as not bothered how the team is getting on.

Be honest

Communication is not much use if your team believes it is not getting the whole picture. Bad news is still news, and you must trust that your people are mature enough to handle it, or you may find they are insulted and no longer believe what you tell them. This does not mean shouting every piece of office gossip from the rooftop, but it does mean keeping your team abreast of all that is pertinent to them.

Consultation

Effective consultation is a vital tool to improving performance. Your team members have specific roles. Your collective overview may be more knowledgeable, but there may be team members whose specific knowledge is greater than yours. Asking for their opinion is not weak; it is sensible, and it serves to empower that team member. The more facts you have, the easier and more effective your decision-making will be. Getting the most out of your team is greatly aided by effective consultation and it demonstrates respect from you to them.

Training

Training is a boon if it is relevant to the team members receiving it. You are guaranteed to alienate staff by sending them on courses that bear no relevance to their role. Training for the sake of training is counter-productive. You need to ask: Will the training help the business? Is it geared to the priorities of the business? Are the right individuals and teams within your organization receiving the training? How can I quantify any improvement?

Training must be organized and delivered effectively or you should not commit to it in the first place. Ensure that the agreed priorities are met. Once this happens, think how you can help individual team members in their personal development. This can be a real aid towards improving performance and motivation.

When the training is over, try and evaluate its worth. Where do you expect to see improvements? If you evaluate effectively, you can judge where further investment in training will pay off.

Organizations of all sizes invest in their people through effective training. Your team is your most valuable asset and their performance has an impact on the company's bottom line.

All companies should review performance of their staff on a regular basis. When staff appraisals do not work, it is for the following reasons: There is no system in place for undertaking reviews on a regular basis; there is no paper trail to follow so people don't know where to start; they are used purely to air grievances so become a negative thing; the appraiser isn't trained to appraise so the results are unreliable; there is no follow-up so improvements are missed.

10 WAYS TO BE A BETTER LEADER

1. Ask to be judged

Finding out what others think of your leadership skills can really help you change for the better. Sometimes leaders can be so wrapped up in appraising others, that they do not seek appraisal from below, only from their own superiors. Your team is the best source of feedback, because they are on the receiving end of your "skills" every day. Honesty should be encouraged, but bear in mind that it may only be anonymous feedback that holds the truth if your team believes you are going to use it against them, or become defensive about what they say. If you have created a trusting and open environment, this should not be a problem.

2. Don't abuse your power

If people are questioning why certain things are done, or the logic of decisions, never pull rank in response. Your team should feel empowered, if only by you taking the time to explain the rationale for any decisions that have been made. Your team must be on your side. This will not happen by you telling them that the decision is the right one because you are the boss. Your team may not agree, but they should know why a situation is how it is.

3. Your team is intelligent and can be trusted

Your team should be allowed to take actions and make decisions. Trust is a vital component of leadership skills. If you can't trust people to do their jobs, then you have the wrong people, or you're not managing them properly. Let them do what they are there to do without peering over their shoulders every fifteen minutes, asking what they are doing with their time.

4. Listen

Truly listening to your team is one of the greatest leadership skills. Good listeners come across as genuinely interested, empathetic, and concerned to find out what's going on. All great leaders have great communication skills.

Unhappy team members can only exist where their problems have not been aired. Create an environment where problems can be discussed so that solutions can be found.

5. Stop being an expert on everything

Leaders often achieve their positions by being proficient in a certain area, and thus will have an opinion on how to fix problems. They believe it's better to tell someone what to do, or even to do it themselves, than give their team the opportunity to develop their own solutions, and therefore exercise their creativity.

6. Be constructive

Negativity breeds negativity. How you communicate has a profound effect on your team, as a whole and individually. Criticisms will always need to be made by leaders, but try to make them constructive, and deliver them without emotional attachment.

7. Judge your success by your team's

The true success of a leader can be measured by the success of the people who work for them. You cannot be a successful leader of a failing team, just as you cannot be a successful general of a defeated army. Your focus should always be on building your team's skills and removing obstacles in their way.

8. Don't be a narcissist

Nothing is more annoying for team members than leaders who make their decisions based on how good it will make them appear to their superiors. A key leadership skill is integrity. Integrity is about doing the right thing, and allowing praise where praise is due, even if that is not at your door.

9. Have a sense of humor

People work better when they are enjoying themselves. The work itself may be dull, but the environment doe not have to be. Stifling fun also means stifling creativity. Team members love it when the leader joins in and has fun. This does not have to create a flippant atmosphere; on the contrary, this is a tenet of team-building.

10. Don't be too distant

Without revealing you innermost secrets, it is possible for leaders to show a more human side. If mutual respect exists, this should not be seen as vulnerability, rather a sign that you are a sentient human being, just as your team members are. Only when your team gets to know the real you will the true foundations of good leadership be properly established – trust and respect.

CONCLUSION

Sun Tzu, writing in the 5th century BC in *The Art of War* said: "What enables the wise sovereign and the good general to strike and conquer and achieve things beyond the reach of ordinary men is *foreknowledge*."

This is an as-yet-unmentioned attribute of a great leader – the ability to predict. No matter how many managerial and people skills the business leader possesses, they will all be jeopardized if he or she cannot anticipate the effects of the plans they put in place, and the actions they take. In this respect, it may be that their age and experience must take precedence over consultation with the "troops", who may little understand the ramifications of what is about to take place.

This is where the genuine leader comes to the fore and truly claims their title. When all around are scratching their heads and reluctant to make a decision, old-style leadership must come into play. The modern leader may utterly fail in this scenario for lack of guts and an over-familiarity with their team.

As Sun Tzu says: "Some leaders are generous but cannot use their men. They love their men but cannot command them... These leaders create spoiled children. Their soldiers are useless."

Leadership may have become a different beast over the years, but it is still, at its heart, about *leading*.

With the help of this eBook you too can become a great leader. By following the leadership principles within you will be respected for your fairness, your skills and your ability to lead people in a humane but necessary way to achieve greatness with your team.

Leading people can be one of the most rewarding things you've ever done if you do it right. Do it wrong, and leadership can quickly become a nightmare you hope to wake up from sooner than later.

I trust you enjoyed learning from **Leadership - Becoming a Better Leader** and look forward to seeing you succeed.

Printed by Libri Plureos GmbH in Hamburg, Germany